*R*ELIGION
and
*D*ISABILITY

Religion and Disability

Essays in Scripture, Theology and Ethics

Marilyn E. Bishop, editor

Sheed & Ward
Kansas City

Sheed & Ward™ is a service of The National Catholic Reporter Publishing Company.

⸻⸻⸻◆⸻⸻⸻

Library of Congress Cataloguing-in-Publication Data

Religion and disability : essays in Scripture, theology, and ethics / Marilyn E. Bishop, ed.
       p.   cm.
    Includes bibliographical references.
    ISBN: 1-55612-713-8 (alk. paper)
    1. Church work with the handicapped. 2. Handicapped—Biblical teaching. 3. Handicapped—Religious life. I. Bishop, Marilyn.
BV4460.R45   1995
261.8'324—dc20   94-44885
                                             CIP

⸻⸻⸻◆⸻⸻⸻

Published by: Sheed & Ward
                115 E. Armour Blvd.
                P.O. Box 419492
                Kansas City, MO 64141

To order, call: (800) 333-7373

Contents

Foreword

This book is both a collection of interrelated theological ideas from several very knowledgeable people and a rationale for a new direction in seminary formation based on these ideas and experiences. Let me explain.

Years of ministry with disabled people have demonstrated to my colleagues and me that our churches, created to be havens of love and support, have, in reality, often become towering edifices of rejection, both physically and environmentally. Disabled people are absent from our church congregations partly because of the physical structure of those churches, but especially because of the prejudice and discomfort attributable in large part to the absence of education at the seminary level about both the ways and the "whys" involved in welcoming people who are different, people who apparently do not fit into the structures of creed, belief and ritual.

For many years, professionals, parents and people who are disabled have tried to educate and inform those in ministry about "how it could be." But, we all learned, disability was yet another "issue," one that is not to be given time in a crowded seminary curriculum. We in this ministry continue to teach when and where we can about the giftedness of this population we call disabled, but our efforts remain in the "extracurricular" category.

Yet, we know that the theological challenge that disability brings is not a minor religious problem. It is a pivotal question with which our theologians have struggled, searching for the meaning of differentness in our religious belief system. This was a question for the faculty in our seminaries and schools of theology to wrestle. And this "wrestling" needs to take place in a public forum where seminary professors come to understand and then to take ideas and convictions back to their classrooms for further expansion.

This was the idea born at a National Council of Churches' Committee on Disabilities discussion with Lew Merrick (Presbyterian), Dennis Busse (Lutheran), Ted Verseput (Christian Reformed Church in North America) and myself (Roman Catholic). The result was a symposium sponsored by the Center for Ministry with Disabled People of the University of Dayton: "Ministry Perspectives on Disability: Theology, Scripture and Ethics," at Bergamo Center in Dayton, Ohio in March 1994.

Three world-renowned men, each known for his scholarship and prestige in the world of theological schools, gathered to deliver their thoughts about disability. Each presenter spoke from the background of his scholarship and his lived experience with disability.

About the Presenters

Donald Senior is a Passionist priest and a professor of New Testament Studies at Catholic Theological Union in Chicago. Fr. Senior was appointed president of this seminary in 1988 and continues to serve in that capacity.

Fr. Senior received his doctorate in New Testament Studies from the University of Louvain. He has authored 16 books, is coeditor of a 22-volume international commentary series entitled, *New Testament Message*, and is associate editor of *The Bible Today* and *New Theology Review*. For eight years he was director of the schools' Israel Study Program, which included a biannual journey to the Holy Land with a group of people with disabilities. Part of Fr. Senior's education came from his sister, Miriam, who has mental retardation.

Fr. Senior's presentation, "Beware of the Canaanite Woman: Disability and the Bible," delves into the deepest currents of biblical thought to offer insight into the truth of what it means to be a human being and a child of God. His study takes the reader from the attitude-producing rules set down by the patriarchal fathers' attempt to create order out of chaos to the leap of Jesus Christ who broke boundaries to foster a society of love rather than restrictions. According to Fr. Senior, it is in the scriptures that we encounter the disabled person who dares to believe that through the power of God community is truly possible.

John Macquarrie is an Anglican priest, a former army chaplain and university professor, and an author, a husband, and a father. He is a graduate of the University of Glasgow, where he earned a Ph.D., and of Oxford University of Cambridge, where he received a doctorate in divinity. Now retired, Fr. Macquarrie was a professor of systematic theology at Union Theological Seminary in New York and a Lady Margaret Professor of Divinity at the University of Oxford. Since 1955, Dr. Macquarrie has authored 23 books, edited three additional ones, and has received six honorary Ph.D. degrees throughout the world.

In "Theological Reflections on Disability," Dr. Macquarrie joins the understanding of disability which he gained from his son, who has autism, with his ability to think and reflect theologically. Here we are invited to consider whether any person can ever be described as a "thing." With a basic understanding of what makes one human, Dr. Macquarrie leads us to applications of his theology which make sense in a world that is tempted to disregard and even destroy a person who, by today's standards, is nonproductive and, therefore, useless.

Stanley Hauerwas is professor of theological ethics at The Divinity School of Duke University. Dr. Hauerwas received four degrees, including his doctorate, from Yale University. He was a member of the faculty at Notre Dame for 14 years. In 1984 he joined the faculty at Duke University, where he served as director of graduate studies for 6 years.

His authorship of 12 books, editorship of five books and his many lectures have focused on political theory, medical ethics, the care of people with mental retardation, and questions of war and peace. He considers himself to be a theologian rather than an ethicist. Yet, his chapter, "The Church and Mentally Handicapped Persons," fits under the definition of ethics as "the principles of conduct governing an individual or group." He has for many years referred to the lives of persons with mental retardation in order to examine how Christian convictions have shaped the response of the congregation to people who are mentally retarded. He does this by emphasizing the church as a community shaped by story.

Dr. Hauerwas challenges us to imagine a world where the church community envelops the person with mental retardation in such a way that that person is cared about as a resource of creative, joyful, gospel life.

It is from these men that we can take hope for the future of education within the seminary structure. It is their example that can be used by faculty everywhere to dare to ask the question about the meaning and implication of disability in all facets of religion: theology, ethics, scripture, Christian education, Church history, administration, pastoral care, liturgy, and architecture. Any course within our seminaries and schools of theology would be enriched by including the relationship between the course of study and the question: "Are we as Christians welcoming all of God's people or are we welcoming only those who fit the system and turning away those who don't?"

As always, in the planning, preparation, and producing of any event, whether it be a symposium or the resulting publication, there are many people who contribute their gifts. Among those who have assisted are Fr. Joseph Kozar, S.M., (University of Dayton); Newell Wert, Ph.D., (United Theological Seminary); Peter Chmielewski (Dayton, OH resident); Fr. James Heft, S.M., (University of Dayton), and Margaret Shufflebarger, secretary, bookkeeper, and typist. We thank them all for their belief in the need to bring the topic of disability to the forefront.

Marilyn Bishop, Director
Center for Ministry with Disabled People
University of Dayton
June, 1994

Religion and Disability

Essays in Scripture, Theology and Ethics

—— *1* ——

Beware of the Canaanite Woman: Disability and the Bible

Donald Senior, C.P.

The Bible comes alive when it is brought into contact with genuine human experience. The biblical materials are not the proceedings of an academic symposium but the narratives, proverbial wisdom, songs and laments that sprang from the human and religious yearnings of a people.

This can be stated in a more formal and technical way if related to recent developments in biblical hermeneutics. Historical critical methodology, as one dominant mode of scientific exegesis, is undergoing something of an identity crisis in recent years. The exaggerated claims to objectivity and dispassionate analysis of the biblical text on the part of some of its proponents has run aground on the experience of many who believe their particular perspective has been overlooked or discounted by the purveyors of scientific historical criticism. Thus

1

liberation theologians accuse European and North American exegetes of reading the biblical text from the vantage point of an economically and socially dominant culture. Feminists approach the biblical text with the formal "suspicion" that the bible and its traditional interpreters operate from the bias of a patriarchal viewpoint.

Allied to this is a complementary emphasis that stresses not only historical interests concerning the origin of the text and its original milieu but also the relationship between the text and the reader. At stake in interpreting the Bible are not only the original milieu and intention of the biblical authors, but the dynamic of the text itself and its impact on the reader.

Pastoral contexts can supply the vital juices for these types of hermeneutical discussions, making them much more than explorations of methodology but a life-giving encounter with the Word of God. And I would like to make the case that the experience of physical and mental disability—and the attendant impact on a human community—is precisely the kind of profound human and religious experience that provides a crucial and religiously fruitful vantage point for biblical interpretation.

Why Disability?

Is the experience of physical or mental disability on a par with economic oppression or sexism? Does it represent, in other words, a valid perspective from which to interpret the Bible? I am convinced that it does.

First of all, it is evident that disability is a pervasive and profound human experience, transcending categories of economic class, cultural background, or gender. The sheer number of persons with disabilities will only increase as health care improves and becomes more widely available. From the point of view of ministry, there are few, if any, congregations that do not include members with a variety of overt and hidden disabilities. In simple pragmatic terms, anyone who is preparing to be a teacher, preacher, pastor, or counselor in congregations today needs to understand and be sensitive to the experience of persons with disabilities.

Also, theological schools and seminaries should be accessible to students with disabilities who feel a call to ministry. Obviously, this is not just a matter of having a ramp to the front entrance but of being hospitable in every sense of the word to the experience of a disabled student.

In very practical terms, how sensitive will future ministers be to language when, for example, the Bible translations calls those who are mobility-impaired "crippled?" Or, how will one preach in the presence of someone with a destroyed optic nerve on a gospel story in which Jesus heals a person blind from birth? Or what do we make of the point so emphatically made by some religious people that illness is caused by sin or lack of faith? How, for example, should one preach on the story of the healing of the paralytic whose sin Jesus forgives before healing the man and seems to make the two actions equivalent? And what about the proper role of someone with a very visible and severe physical limitation who feels a vocational call to lead worship, or someone with a severe speech impediment who wishes to be a lector? And, an even more profound challenge, what about those who are mentally ill or have severe developmental disabilities and seem to have no prospects for meaningful human accomplishment?

But, as in the case of liberation and feminist perspectives, the issue goes much further than attentiveness to an overlooked or marginalized constituency. I am convinced that the experiences that surround disability—both for the disabled persons and their communities—have profound connections to the deepest currents of biblical thought. Disability, as I will attempt to illustrate, touches directly on the question of a community's identity, on the meaning of transformation and redemption, indeed, on the very image we have of God within the Christian faith.

All of these are issues that occur and reoccur within the Old and New Testaments. To understand more deeply the experience of a person with a disability will not only help sensitize a minister—particularly one who is able-bodied—to the experiences of a significant number of people in any given community but can also offer insight into the very truth of what it means to be a human being and a child of God.

Entry Points

I would like to illustrate what I mean by looking at several aspects of the experience of disability which I believe have profound connections to currents within the biblical world. Within the time limits of the symposium, I will not be able to deal with them in an exhaustive way, but hopefully the imperatives for dealing with the experience of disability within a theological curriculum will be clear.

Healing and Community Self-Definition

For people who have made the commitment to join in a symposium such as this, the fact that exclusion and access are major issues for persons with disabilities needs little emphasis. I am speaking, of course, not just about physical obstacles that exclude one from participation in the community—the steps, the narrow doors, the absence of braille or interpreters, the insufficiency of public transportation—but attitudinal ones: the fear, the ignorance, the patronization, the prejudice that block many people with disabilities from their rightful place within the community.

These experiences are not simply inconveniences or mere documentation of human insensitivity. The right to participation in one's community touches on issues of justice and, ultimately, concerns one's dignity as a child of God. Conversely, exclusion from the community to which one belongs can cause acute suffering and can erode a person's sense of identity.

Viewed from this perspective, the recent enactment of the Americans with Disabilities Act (ADA) was not simply a victory for civil rights on behalf of disabled citizens, but has profound theological meaning as well. As has more than once been the case, movements within what we call secular society can be more alert to issues of justice than the church. Although many religious people were certainly involved, the pressure to insure civil rights for people with disabilities did not begin with the churches but primarily with activists within the disabled community. Perhaps a similar case could be made about women's rights and, much earlier, the crusade against slavery.

The recent U.S. Bishops' letter on the economy, *Economic Justice for All*—drawing on a long tradition of Catholic social thought—does, to its credit, emphasize that inclusion within the social and political community is an issue of justice fundamental to the Gospel. Exclusion, on the other hand, has an oppressive, dehumanizing impact running contrary to the Christian vision. The Bishops' letter applied the category of inclusion to such issues as employment and rights of workers rather than to the experience of disabled people, but the structure of thought is the same.

The categories of inclusion and exclusion touch immediately on a profound current of biblical thought. The root meaning of justice in the biblical context has to do with right relationships, with "the restoration of a situation or environment which promotes equity and harmony in a community" (*Anchor Bible Dictionary*). The biblical vision of *shalom* evidenced in a text such as Isaiah 65: 17-25 views the eschatological Israel as one in which death is defeated and all are at peace. All find satisfaction in the work of their hands, and no one—except the unjust—are excluded.

One could, in fact, replay much of the saga of Israel as a saga of justice, as an attempt to build a community reflective of covenant values, a movement from death and oppression in Egypt to one of identity and belonging in a God-given land.

Every community, of course, needs boundaries in order to have a sense of identity and purpose. Within the course of Israel's history, as played out in the biblical epic, it is the king and the priests who become the guardians of community boundaries, who are, in effect, the gatekeepers of Israelite identity. Within the monarchical and priestly traditions of the biblical literature, that identity is symbolized ultimately both in the throne of David and the Temple with its cult. Here one ritualized access to the ultimate center of Israel's identity, the presence of the living God in Zion. Access to this sacred center was reserved for those purified of death and its symptoms, for those who exemplified the values of the covenant. Through such well-defined cultic boundaries, Israel attempted to define the sacred order of reality and to stave off chaos and fragmentation.

The prophetic movements, on the other hand, represent a certain counterweight to the necessary but sometimes deadly self-defining emphasis of priest and king when the formal structures of identity are pressed without concern for the underlying values. When the values of the covenant—justice, compassion, integrity—are violated, particularly by the leadership, then the prophetic critique is directed against the boundary-defining symbols of king, priest, temple and cult. In the scorching indictment of Isaiah, chapter 1, God wearies of the Temple and its cult, and the community is commanded: "Cease to do evil; seek justice, rescue the oppressed, defend the orphan and plead for the widow" (Isaiah 1:12-17). Justice and inclusion become, ultimately, more crucial to the identity of the people than the defining symbols of temple and cult.

Defining what is "clean" or "unclean" or "pure" or "impure" within the cultic society of ancient Israel is a difficult issue that resists simplification. Yet by any definition it surely has connections with the issue of boundaries and community identification: the boundary between life and death, between what is known and what is strange; between what belongs and what is judged foreign or alien. Along with a host of other entities, bodily disability was often considered an indication of cultic impurity (not to be confused immediately with moral impurity). Therefore, those with certain overt disabilities were denied access to at least the most visible and public zone of inclusion in a sacred society—the inner courts of the temple—and were considered not eligible to be Levites.

The infamous text of Leviticus 21:16-23 spells this out:

> . . . No one of your offspring throughout their generations who has a blemish may approach to offer the food of his God. For no one who has a blemish shall draw near, one who is blind or lame, or one who has a mutilated face or a limb too long, or one who has a broken foot or a broken hand, or a hunchback, or a dwarf, or a man with a blemish in his eyes or an itching disease or scabs or crushed testicles. No descendant of Aaron the priest who has a blemish shall come near to offer the Lord's offerings by fire; since he has a blemish, he shall not come near to offer the food of his God. He may eat the food of his God, of the most holy as well of the holy. But he shall not come near to the curtain or approach the altar, because he has a blemish, that he may not profane my sanctuaries; for I am the Lord; I sanctify them." (This text was explicitly cited as a biblical warrant for the notion of impediments to ordination that were part of the Roman Catholic Canon law until the mid 1980s.)

What I am describing as an underlying dynamic of ancient Israel is, evidently, one of the keys to understanding the conflict and tension that surrounded Jesus' own mission as presented in the gospel literature, particularly his association with the marginalized and his healing ministry. In the chronic tension between cultic self-definition and prophetic critique, Jesus' healings become flashpoints on the frontier.

As Gerd Theissen in his important work on the miracles stories noted, one of the characteristic features of the gospel healing narratives is the element of boundary crossing. The action of Jesus in touching the flesh of the leper in Mark 1:41 represents not only a characteristic gesture of healing but an act of solidarity, bridging the chasm between the leper and the healer, crossing the boundary between life and death so clearly staked out in Leviticus 13 concerning leprosy. Jesus' liberation of the woman bent double in Luke 13, his naming her a "daughter of Abraham," and his vigorous defense of her against the attack of the synagogue manager are actions that not only effect physical transformation but, equally important, draw the woman into the center of the synagogue community.

Surely it is not coincidental that all of Jesus' encounters with Gentiles take place in the context of healings. Some of these stories are the cure of the Syro-Phoenician woman's daughter across the borders of Tyre and Sidon (Mk 7:24-30), the release of the Garadene from the demonic power named Legion on the other side of the sea and in the region of the Decapolis (Mk 5:1-20), and the healing with a word of the centurion's servant (Mt 8:5-13). All of these represent profound crossing of boundaries through which the Gospels begin to redefine the scope of Jesus' ministry and, thereby, to redefine the borders of the rule of God.

While on one level the healing stories display the messianic power of Jesus to heal, and thereby have inherent christological meaning, on another level they are ecclesiological stories, defining who belongs to the kingdom of God or, in another set of language, defining the inclusive nature of the eschatological community of Israel. Through such actions Jesus was fashioning a revitalized community of Israel. His boundary crossing mission to Tyre and Sidon and to Gadara were harbingers of the mission of the post-Easter community when the boundaries of the community would include Gentiles as well as Jews.

This inherently inclusive thrust of Jesus' healing ministry is demonstrated by the fact that the vocabulary of healing is extended to incidents of inclusion in which no physical transformation takes place. In Mark's account of the call of Levi (2:14-17), Jesus defends his association with outcasts and sinners by quoting a proverb that, in effect, defines his inclusive ministry: "Those who are well have no need of a physician, but those who are sick: I have come to call not the righteous but sinners." Similarly in Luke's account of Jesus' inaugural preaching in the synagogue of Nazareth, Jesus evokes the healing ministries of Elijah who brought food to the widow at Zarephath in Sidon and that of Elisha who cleansed the leprosy of Naaman the Syrian. In so doing, Jesus challenged the narrow perspective of his hometown community: "Doubtless you will quote to me this proverb, 'Doctor, cure yourself. Do here in your hometown the things that we have heard you did at Capernaum'" (Lk 4:23). In these instances healing becomes a metaphor for the inclusion of people with disabilities, the Gentile and the tax collector into the Kingdom of God.

Thus through his healing ministry, not unlike the prophetic critiques of an Amos, Isaiah or Jeremiah, Jesus challenges the prescribed boundaries of God's people and demands access on behalf of those who have been excluded. The act of healing and transformation becomes an act of solidarity and inclusion.

Healing and Community Transformation

The healing ministry of Jesus not only enabled those who were on the periphery the opportunity to enter the heart of the community, it also served to transform the community itself. A friend of mine who is physically disabled protested to me about using the gospel healing stories as stories of inclusion because those who are sick and disabled seem to gain access to the community only after they are cured. Thus, in effect, disabled people gain access to the community but only on the terms of the able-bodied.

Her observation is a significant one and reminds us to keep in mind another important aspect of the healing stories in the Gospels. Transformation is not reserved to those who are sick or disabled. In fact, in most of the gospel stories both the person healed by Jesus and the community itself undergo profound transformation.

A helpful distinction in analyzing the gospel materials is that between "curing" and "healing." I use the term "cure" in a strict physical sense, referring to physical transformation by which, for example, the withered arm of the man in the synagogue of Capernaum is made straight. "Healing" has a more profound and comprehensive meaning, referring not only to physical transformation but to a profound spiritual transformation as well. Not all people—even in the drama of the Gospels—have access to cure; but all are invited to be healed. Even Jesus himself, one could say, would ultimately not experience cure but would be healed through the experience of resurrection.

Viewed in this more profound sense, the healing stories in the Gospels become transformation or redemption stories, transformation that often affects the community as well as the individual.

The social or communitarian dimension that is involved in most instances of authentic healing stands out when the experience of serious illness or the trauma associated with physical disability is viewed as a "liminal" experience—an analysis made popular through the work of Victor Turner.

Illness or the experience associated with disability is seldom a static reality but a dynamic narrative, a process with a beginning, a middle, and an end. The person who becomes seriously ill or has a disabling accident, for example, finds that, in effect, they leave one world and set out for a new one. The "world" that they had known changes: their relationship to their body, to their family or community, to their work—all of these may change radically. As the illness progresses, the sick or disabled person may find themselves on the threshold between two worlds—in a truly "liminal" state. They have left one familiar world and have not yet entered another—a world to be defined possibly through rehabilitation or cure, or through entry into death. Being on this threshold between two worlds often imposes on the person who is sick or injured a sense of profound isolation.

Even if the person experiences cure or rehabilitation and returns to their family or community, in a sense they cannot "come home again" because they have changed profoundly. And here is where conflict with the community of the "healthy" can often occur. The community to which the sick or disabled person returns may not recognize the profound transformation that has taken place. They are not aware that the person they welcome back is returning from a journey that has changed their life forever. As a result, conflicts can easily develop.

This is why many of the gospel stories give attention not only to the moment of healing itself but to the social reinsertion that follows. Thus the leper, when cleansed by Jesus, is urgently instructed to go and give testimony of his cure to the priests—because in Leviticus 14 only the priests could declare a leper cleansed and permit his return to the community. In the story of the man born blind in chapter 9 of John's Gospel, the physical cure of the blind man occupies only a small portion of the narrative; the real attention is on the resistance of the Pharisees to accept the transformation that has taken place in this man. In Luke's account of the woman bent double, the synagogue manager is concerned only with the violation of the Sabbath and cannot see this woman's newfound dignity as a daughter of Abraham.

The Bible is aware that letting the "outsider" in often involves transformation for the insider as well. Perhaps no more dramatic example of this can be found than in the story of the Canaanite woman in Matthew 15:21-28. Here resistance to change is demonstrated not by the stereotyped opponents of Jesus but by Jesus himself. The woman's plea on behalf of her daughter is met first with silence, then with Jesus' statement that he was sent "only to the lost sheep of the house of Israel," and, finally, with apparent insult, as Jesus declares, "It is not fair to take the children's food and throw it to the dogs." The woman's fierce determination to find healing for her daughter and her persistent assault of Jesus' own boundaries finally break through. While the woman's daughter is healed, the story also dares to suggest that Jesus himself is transformed: once he has given way to the tenacious demand for healing on the part of the Canaanite woman, no longer is his mission only to the lost sheep of the house of Israel!

Healing and Empowerment

Our North American culture is currently fascinated with issues of abuse and victimization. The impact of exclusion and negative attitudes on those with disabilities is not, however, a passing fad: truly, our society can victimize those with disabilities.

This can take place in a number of often subtle ways. For example, people are depersonalized by identifying them through their disability (the blind man; the woman with the limp; a spastic son). Or a person with a disability can be treated as less than human or ignored as if not present, such as when a clerk in a store gives the change to the able-bodied attendant of a customer using a wheelchair rather than the disabled adult who paid for the item. Further, it is humiliating to be limited to entering a church or public building only through a back door or a freight elevator, or worse—having to be carried. Then there are the quiet but very real penalties that make it impossible for someone to be employed if they want to retain their insurance. Or, when someone is employed, the constant struggle to be taken seriously and with respect by employer or coworkers.

Or in a different key, the disabled person can be labeled as "different" and idealized as very "special," as having unique powers or spiritual capacities. All of these have the impact of viewing persons with disability in a one-dimensional fashion and of isolating or marginalizing them within the community.

In some instances, a particular culture can attach a symbolic dimension to certain illnesses or disabilities, giving them the aura of death itself. Susan Sontag, for example, has traced the manner in which tuberculosis, then cancer, and now AIDS all have taken on a highly charged symbolic dimension in Western societies in which those who suffered from such illnesses were considered the "living dead," their conditions a matter of shame.

As a result of such societal responses, people who are disabled can, in effect, be "schooled" to absorb and accept the destructive judgments implicit in such societal attitudes. The person who is sick may feel profound guilt about their condition. Or they may be encouraged—often by well-meaning religious people—to see their condition as a result of their own sinfulness or the deficiency of their faith. Another approach that people with disabilities experience from the church is encouragement to be "passive"—that is, to accept their condition and to "offer it up" as a sacrifice for sin, to see themselves as sacrificial victims rather than as active participants in the mission of the church. Certainly the attitude of bearing illness in a spirit of faith and even seeing it as somehow redemptive is an authentic Christian response. However, it is not the only Christian response, and in some instances would be inadequate. Persons with disabilities also have rights they should demand and protect. They also have responsibilities as Christians to take up a mission of transformation no matter what a person's capacity may be.

Here, too, is found an entry into the biblical world, particularly in the gospel healing stories. In his work referred to earlier, Theissen notes within the miracle stories two basic kinds of elements:

one of which he calls "boundary crossing" and the other "boundary stressing." Boundary "stressing" elements are those realities or people which emphasize the impenetrable boundary between the sick and the healthy, between those on the inside and those excluded, between the clean and the unclean, between the living and the dead. The din of the crowd that prevents Bartimaeus' pleas from reaching Jesus' ears; the able-bodied friends who crowd the door of Simon's house, forcing the paralytic and his friends to enter through the roof; the anger of the synagogue manager because the woman bent double had come to be healed on the Sabbath; the Pharisees' condemnation of Jesus' association with outcasts and sinner—these are some of the elements within the stories that reinforce the boundary.

Other elements, however, are boundary "crossing" features. Jesus the healer is the most evident boundary crossing dynamic in the stories—reaching to touch the leper, catching the cry of the blind Bartimaeus, feeling the touch of the woman with the hemorrhage, going across the sea to reach the Gadarene or, with a word, healing the son of the centurion.

But often those who are sick are boundary crossers as well. The woman with the hemorrhage dares to touch the tassel of Jesus' cloak, even though the law commanded her not to pollute others with her flow of blood. The leper comes and kneels before Jesus, even though Leviticus warned the lepers not to approach any living being (Lev

13:45-46). The friends of the paralytic take the roof off in order to bring their friend to Jesus, refusing to be denied entrance by the able-bodied that block the doorway.

This determination to seek the source of life is frequently labeled "faith" in the healing stories. It is the faith of the paralytic friends which moves Jesus to raise him from his pallet; it is the faith of Bartimaeus that enables him to see. Faith in this instance is no mere conviction that Jesus has the power to heal but the active determination to brave crossing the boundary and reach him.

No gospel story illustrates this dynamic more vividly than the story of the Canaanite woman. In this case, Jesus himself takes the role of the boundary "stresser"; his silence, the narrow scope of this mission, and his rebuff to the woman all serve to emphasize the boundary between this Gentile woman and the children of Israel. Her fierce parental love for her ill daughter drives her to challenge Jesus and to cross any boundary he guards. As Jesus notes at the end of the story, "Woman, great is your faith! Let it be done for you as you wish." (Mt 15:28).

Theissen goes on to define the Gospel miracles as "protests against the merely rational"; that is, the miracle stories are "revelation stories" that disclose possibilities for life and communion not apparent to a merely reasonable analysis of reality. Ironically, the religious leaders—who should by definition be most attuned to the transcendent realities—become champions of limits by stressing boundaries and rationality. Those who are sick or disabled and who refuse to remain passive dare to believe that through the power of God the boundaries can be crossed and communion can be found.

Healing as Revelation

These examples illustrate some of the profound and extensive symmetry between the experience of disability and substantial concerns of the biblical message. Issues such as incorporation within the covenant community, respect for the dignity of the defenseless, and the redemption transformation involved for both community and individual in the healing process stand at the center of biblical theology in both Old and New Testaments.

One could push this even further. The christological message of the healing stories in the synoptic tradition and, even more evidently in John, suggests that the healing stories which embody in varying degrees the motifs we have discussed are also "revelation" stories, vehicles that disclose the fundamental reality of God's relationship to humanity. Jesus' compassion, commitment to justice, attentiveness to those on the margin, and drive to gather even devalued children of Israel are understood in the logic of the New Testament to be not only disclosures about Jesus but, ultimately, about God. In the language of John's Gospel, the healing stories are "signs" that reveal the presence of God incarnate in the word Jesus. Thus there is an explicit theodicy in the healing mission of Jesus.

In Matthew 15:29-31, the sight of the great crowds who stream to Jesus for healing on the mountain-top in Galilee prompts the witnesses to "praise the God of Israel" who is thus manifested in the powerful compassion of Jesus. In response to the questions of John the Baptist's emissaries whether he was the messiah, Jesus cites his ministry of healing: "Go and tell John what you hear and see: the blind receive their sight, the disabled walk, lepers are cleansed, the deaf hear, the dead are raised, and the poor have good news brought to them" (Mt 11:4-5). The casting out of demons and healings are "signs" that the rule of God is at hand. In Acts 3:1-10, for example, the healing of the paralyzed man who begged at the gate called "Beautiful" ends with his leap like a stag within the temple courtyard. This evokes Isaiah's dream of Israel in the final age when all would be healed by God's redemptive power, "opening the eyes of the blind, unstopping the ears of the deaf, and enabling the lame to leap like a stag and the tongue of the speechless to sing for joy" (Is 35:5-6).

For Pauline theology, the redemptive process of moving from death to life, from exclusion to inclusion, from alienation to forgiveness reveals the mission of Jesus and the nature of God. The paschal mystery stands at the very center of Paul's theology. The experience of what Paul calls bodily "weakness" or illness (*asthenia*) helps him to elaborate his profound "wisdom of the Cross."

Paul is convinced that God's power works through human weakness, through the "dying" of his own body. This paradoxical wisdom of the cross which is "a scandal to the Jews and foolishness to Greeks" (1 Cor 1:23) is based on the startling reality disclosed to Paul in his experience of the risen Christ: namely, that God chose to redeem the world through a crucified Messiah. This unexpected revelation causes Paul to look in a new way at the history of Israel and at his own religious convictions, and ultimately leads him to the discovery of his God-given mission to proclaim the Gospel to the Gentiles.

The paschal mystery whereby God's power moves Jesus from death to life becomes, in a sense, the divine optic, through which Paul sees all of human experience and all of human history in a new way. Paul believes that God is a God of the "ungodly," (Rom 4:5), a God who "gives life to the dead and calls into existence things that do not exist" (Rom 4:17), the God of the crucified Messiah, the God of the Gentiles and the God of sinners. This God is the God of Paul who was born out of due time, who was not a perfect physical specimen, and who certainly knew physical and spiritual weakness due to sin. In Romans 4, where Paul begins to develop this logic of the cross, he alludes to the experience of Abraham who trusted in God even though his own body "was as good as dead" and Sarah's womb was barren (Rom 4:19). God's gift of abundant new life to Abraham and Sarah, even though their physical condition seemed to make it impossible, becomes for Paul a sign of God's paradoxical way of exerting power precisely in and through human "weakness." The definitive experience of this is in the death and resurrection of the crucified Messiah.

How much of Paul's theology was based on his own experience, including the experience of disability? This has long been debated. Are Paul's references to a "thorn in the flesh" in 2 Cor 12:7-10 a reference to an exclusively spiritual or psychological experience? Or does he mean "flesh" quite literally and include a physical dimension?

We may never know the answers to these questions. However, I am inclined to think that Paul had a visible physical disability. This enabled him to develop his theology of the cross in which God's grace enabled him to move from death to life and to accept—even glory—in his weakness. In Galatians 4:13, for example, Paul reminds the Galatians that his physical infirmity enabled him to preach the Gospel to them—as if standing before them with some apparent physical limitation served as a living icon, signifying what the dying and rising of the gospel meant. Paul commends the Galatians for viewing his disability not with "scorn" but as an "angel of God, as Christ Jesus himself" (Gal 4:14).

In 2 Cor 4: 7-12, Paul again states his theology of "weakness."

> But we have this treasure in clay jars, so that it may be made clear that this extraordinary power belongs to God and does not come from us. We are afflicted in every way, but not crushed; perplexed, but not driven to despair; persecuted, but not forsaken; struck

down, but not destroyed; always carrying in the
body the death of Jesus, so that the life of Jesus may also be made visible in our bodies.
For while we live, we are always being given
up to death for Jesus' sake, so that the life of
Jesus may be made visible in our mortal flesh.
So death is at work in us, but life in you.

In Paul's reflections on death and resurrection,
we may reach the profoundest level of New Testament theology and the most daring potential
connection with the experience of people who are
disabled.   The struggle for inclusion, for human
dignity, for generativity by disabled people can be
a sign to the Christian community of the reality of
the Gospel that encompasses all of us.   Some persons with disabilities depend on the support and
care by others for their very existence.   This can
become a sign of how each of us and all of us
stand before the reality of God.

Is this not the implication of Paul's reflections
on the church as the body of Christ in 1 Corin-
thians 12?   I have often asked myself what kind of
a body was Paul thinking about?   The body of
Christ like Adonis—without spot or wrinkle?   Or
was he thinking of the body of the crucified Christ
with its triumphant wounds—the very body that
even the Gospels of Luke and John present as ap-
pearing to the disciples in the wake of the resurrection?   Paul's own words indicate that he has in
mind the crucified body when speaking of the
church, a body in which those

> . . . members which seem to be weaker are
> indispensable, and those members of the body

that we think less honorable we clothe with greater honor, and our less respectable members are treated with greater respect. God has so arranged the body, giving the greater honor to the inferior member that there may be no dissension within the body, but the members may have the same care for one another. If one member suffers, all suffer together with it; if one member is honored, all rejoice together with it.

A body that despises or overlooks its own members is an unhealthy body. A church that is not inclusive of people who are disabled is incomplete and is not yet the body of the crucified and risen Christ.

Conclusion

It has not been my intent to bring all of these facets of biblical thought to a satisfactory conclusion, but simply to point out that one taps into these deep biblical currents when one enters the biblical world through the perspective of disability.

It is surely clear that the spectrum of experiences triggered by bodily disability leads to a profound reflection on what it means to be human as well as Christian.

Therefore, dealing with the issue of disability in the context of the Scriptures will never simply be a matter of sensitizing able-bodied students of ministry about the needs and perspectives of the disabled. Nor is it simply a matter of the community as a whole providing access and inclusion for all its members (as wonderful as that prospect might be). But ultimately it is a matter of learning from and being transformed by the vantage point, experience and insight into the meaning of human existence and the Christian message that in many instances persons with disabilities can provide. Put quite simply, the challenge for the church ultimately is not so much to learn how to minister to disabled people but to be open to being ministered to and, ultimately, healed by them. Or, put in gospel language, beware of the Canaanite woman and her daughter.

References

Sontag, S., 1977. *Illness as Metaphor*, New York: Farrar, Straus, and Giroux.

Theissen, G., 1983. *The Miracle Stories of the Early Christian Tradition*, Philadelphia: Fortress.

Turner, V., 1978. *Image and Pilgrimage in Christian Culture: Anthropological Perspectives*, Oxford: Blackwell.

——— 2 ———

Theological Reflections on Disability

John Macquarrie

Human beings differ from inanimate things in several ways, but one of the important ways is that a human being is made up of possibilities which may or may not be realized, whereas a thing comprises a number of fixed properties which make it the kind of things that it is. A knife, for example, is an instrument consisting of a blade attached to a handle, so that it can be used for cutting. Obviously there could be no knife if there were no sharp blade, and even if the handle were missing, one could hardly say that what remained was a knife, however it might be described. When we come to human beings and have to consider possibilities or capacities, the whole situation is far more complicated. A human being has the possibility of sight, and the great majority of people do, in fact, see. But sometimes that possibility is missing or greatly diminished. Where some general human

27

possibility like sight is missing, we speak of handi-cap or disability. Yet we would never think of saying that someone who lacked even such a basic capacity as sight was therefore anything other than a fully human being.

Again, I suppose we could say that any human being has the possibility of making music. But, in fact, many never realize this possibility, though they may try very hard to master a musical instru-ment or to cultivate their voices. However, in such cases we would not normally speak of a handicap or disability. We accept the fact that nature is not egalitarian in distributing abilities, and also that some abilities are more essential to the task of liv-ing than others. To have poor eyesight, for in-stance, would be reckoned a much more serious lack, indeed, a disability, whereas lack of musical skills would certainly be counted a misfortune, but not nearly so serious as blindness, and thus not re-garded as a disability.

Yet both blindness and lack of musical skills are, in very different ways, subtractions from the sum total of human possibilities. One is no doubt much more serious than the other, though both may occasion a great deal of frustration in the per-sons who suffer in these ways. But I think we would also agree that neither of these lacks de-prives the one who suffers from it of his or her essential humanity.

Suppose we tried to visualize the extreme case—that of a human individual who was lacking in all the manifold possibilities of human nature.

In that extreme case, the person would be dead. Yet we still think and speak of a "person," a human being, for we cannot forget that even if the life and all its powers have departed, the deceased was never just a thing. He or she was human and, as we have seen, what is distinctively human is to stand in a wide range of possibilities.

That is why we can never degrade a human being to mere thinghood, for as long as there is life, there is possibility; we still cannot say what that person might become. Even when all natural possibilities have been reduced to the lowest conceivable level, when sight and thought and movement and decision are all in abeyance, for the Christian one has still not come to the point when that person can be written off as nothing or as merely past, for the Christian believes in resurrection, and in the widest sense that simply means that God can still bring forth something new. The God who has wonderfully created human beings with all their possibilities will surely not let that creative energy go to waste, but will bring to fruition the good purpose which has so far been frustrated.

It is hard to see how we could face the grim, disheartening facts of handicap and disability without bringing God into the picture. But is it not the case that these very facts speak against God? For if indeed we claim that this world is the creation of God, and if we claim further that God is good and that the creation is good, how can we square such assertions with the destinies of those men and women who spend a lifetime in an unending battle against some severe handicap or disability? This is, of course, only one part of that wider problem of evil, as we call it, a problem that has plagued theologians for centuries. If there is no God, then there is no problem or, at least, there is no intellectual problem. We just have to accept that this is the way things are because our world is something that has come about through the chance interactions of blind forces. There is then no reason to expect that such a world would be good or specially favorable to human life and its aspirations. But although the intellectual problem would have vanished, the practical or existential problem of coping with disability would remain, and might be even more oppressive if the victims of handicap could no longer expect to find any consolation in a religious faith.

Limitations

Our discussion so far has brought us to face one of the basic truths about human existence, namely, that such an existence is through and through finite. We began by thinking of the human being as constituted by a wide range of possibilities and capacities that might or might not be realized. But before any human being has advanced any distance in the actual business of living, he or she has to recognize that most of these enticing possibilities spread out before us are never going to be realized. In many instances, this may not matter very much, but in some instances it may be an utterly crushing blow to the person concerned. Our lives are constituted not just by wonderful possibilities, but by the hard facts of a world which presents obstacles to their fulfillment and, in the extreme case, might even quench the will to live.

A human being is, in essence, constituted by a contradiction or even a conflict. Such a being is through and through finite.

The powers of such a being are limited: this applies to physical powers. For example, an Olympic champion may run a mile in four minutes, and then new champions may come along and reduce that time by a few seconds. But four minutes minus a few seconds is a barrier that cannot be crossed. The same is true of mental powers. Some very clever persons can solve difficult problems in mathematics and science, but even they have their limits. So it is in everything. And beyond all these various limits there is, for every individual and eventually for the human race, the final limit of death, as far as life in this world is concerned. This unalterable fact of finitude is there, and must be taken into account in any realistic description of what it means to exist in the human condition.

Possibilities

But that is only one side of the picture. The same human being who is hemmed in by finitude is simultaneously reaching out beyond the bound of self, reaching out towards realizing his or her possibilities as an athlete, as a scientist or whatever it may be. Even when the human being strikes against the barriers of finitude, the imagination leaps over them. Human progress in many fields has taken place because men and women were not content to say to themselves, "We've gone as far as we can!" They have pushed the limits further, and sometimes it has even seemed that there are no limits to the advances that the human race can make. And this is where the contradiction or conflict at the heart of our nature clearly emerges. Along with our finitude, there goes a desire for the infinite. Weak and hemmed in as each one of us may be, there is in us (call it by the traditional name of spirit) that leaps out into the infinite realm of being surrounding us.

So humanity is that finite form of being that seeks after the infinite. In the famous words of Pascal, "Man is nothing but a reed, one of the feeblest things in nature; but he is a thinking reed."[1] It is here that we find the origins of religious faith. "Humanity, recognizing its own finitude, looks beyond itself in a quest for the Infinite."[2]

How can we try to understand this extraordinary relationship, a finite being, dependent on all kind of factors outside of itself, yet driven to seek a Being which utterly transcends everything that is finite? Christian theology attempts to answer this question. It goes back to the story of creation, found at the very beginning of the Bible. There we read:

> Then God said, "Let us make man in our image, after our likeness; and let them have dominion over the fish of the sea, and over the birds of the air, and over the cattle, and over all the earth, and over every creeping thing that creeps upon the earth." So God created man in his own image, in the image of God he created him; male and female he created them. (Gen 1: 26-27)

In this teaching, the human being occupies a middle state. Such a being belongs to the created order, it has come from the earth and, as we believe now, has emerged by a long and often painful process of evolution. But this creature is special, because it has within it the image of God, a kind of goal or direction toward which it must strive. It differs from other creatures in the vast range of possibilities which it knows within itself and which, it believes, mirror on the finite level the inconceivably rich being of God.

Purpose

The human destiny is so to cultivate the divine image implanted by God that men and women will themselves grow in likeness to God. But at this point we must be careful to make a distinction. Our destiny is to become like God, not to become God or to usurp the place of God. God remains God, we remain human and therefore creatures. There can be only one infinite Being, for it would be a contradiction to suppose that there could be two infinites existing side by side. Neither of them could be infinite except it had absorbed the other.

To come back for a moment to the biblical creation story: the temptation which the serpent set before Adam and Eve was precisely that they should become "like God" (Gen 3:5). How could this be a temptation and the occasion of their fall into sin, if it was God's intention in creating the human couple that they should bear his image and likeness? The question arises because there is an ambiguity in this expression, "likeness to God." There are some qualities in God which can also be manifested in human beings. Although at the human level they are not identical with what they are in God, they are, nevertheless, analogous. For instance, we believe that "God is love" (1 Jn 4:8). Yet we would also confess that the love of God must be unimaginably deeper and richer than any human love. But this does not rule out the possibility that human love at its best is, on the finite level, "like" the love of God. Indeed, the central Christian doctrine of the incarnation of the eternal Word of God in Jesus Christ implies that the love of Christ on the cross does really reveal to us the love of God the Father for his children. But there are other attributes or qualities of God which belong to his infinitude and which it would be wrong for human beings to emulate. That is why the serpent's suggestion that Adam and Eve should seek to be like God is considered to be a temptation. Human beings, unfortunately, prefer power and possession to love, especially any love that demands self-sacrifice.

Choices

The entire history of the human race, sadly, has been very often like a desperate attempt to usurp the power of God and to take into possession his creation, rather than seeing the human race as the stewards and guardians of creation tending and caring for it in the interests of all the creatures that have a place in it. So though we stand before a great range of possibilities that are presented to us in virtue of our humanity, we cannot and should not embrace them indiscriminately. We cannot because there is no human being who is or ever has been simultaneously a great athlete, a great mathematician, a great painter, a great musician—and we can add as many other such designations as we like. Because of our finitude, in time as well as in ability, we have to choose some possibilities for realization and leave aside others, even though strongly attracted by them. So we cannot embrace all possibilities. But I said not only that we cannot. I add that we should not. We should not because these possibilities have different values. Some lead towards a truly human fulfillment, others can easily lead into sin and the alienation of the self. The pursuit of love is fulfilling; the pursuit of power and possession, if unchecked, leads to the destruction of a truly human self. Therefore in human life we all have to make commitments. We have to divert our energies and our time into some pursuits rather than others. In order to do this, we have to know ourselves, we have to form a realistic idea both of our strengths and our weaknesses.

Of course, only some people, probably a minority, have the luxury of deciding what possibilities they will seek to realize, and what they will let go. In Europe or North America, there is a good deal of choice. But let us suppose you had been born in China. For the overwhelming majority of its billion inhabitants, the pattern of life often is back-breaking work day after day in the paddy fields. There is a sense, therefore, in which a very large number of earth's inhabitants are handicapped, that is to say, unable to realize potentialities which many others take for granted. Indeed, there is a sense in which all are handicapped. There must be very few people who would not have liked to do something or become something, but lacked the possibility. Nevertheless, most people can settle for a limited lifestyle, and even find satisfaction in a few limited activities.

It may be useful to remember that even God seems to have certain limitations. We do speak of God's omnipotence, and there is a verse in the gospels, saying that "with God, all things are possible" (Mark 10, 27). But this does not mean that our Supreme Being is some arbitrary ruler of the universe, who could do anything whatever. God has given to the universe what we call the "laws" of nature and, as far as we can judge, God acts within this lawlike structure. But even if we try to think of God in abstraction from creation, we would still have to acknowledge God's limits. St.

Augustine, believing that God has a rational nature and could not do anything in contradiction to that nature, mentions a whole list of actions, such as telling a lie, which God could not do. St. Thomas also sets limits to what God can do. For instance, God cannot change the past, cannot go back into the past and make an event, once happened, not to have happened. We may think that this is a somewhat speculative assertion, but it does seem to be demanded by what we know about time, and if the past could be changed, we would surely be in a world of absurdity. Admittedly, writers of science fiction seem to do in their novels what even God cannot do, but these writers are working in the realm of fiction, not of reality.

Basis of Self-Esteem

One recognition of the limitation of human capacities is the almost universal phenomenon of "division of labor" in developed economies. In a primitive economy, each individual or head of a family performs all the operations necessary for the maintenance of that family. One person hunts or fishes and perhaps cultivates fruit or vegetables or grain. Another builds the family home, and does anything else that is needed. But in the course of time, people learn that every individual is not equally good at every task. So a point is reached at which each individual recognizes personal strengths, and they exchange their products. One becomes a builder, another a hunter, another a cultivator, and so on. As a society advances and becomes more complicated, the division of labor increases, and now there are thousands of different occupations, each with its peculiar skills. Marx and Engels were critical of the division of labor on the grounds that it separates the worker from the product of his work, and may result in people being condemned to the repetitive performance of monotonous tasks which seem meaningless when lifted out of the process that leads all the way from the raw material to the finished product. But while there may be some force in that objection, it would seem that in a modern industrial society division of labor has become a necessity. It is, however, a mute testimony to the truth that not everybody can do everything, that abilities and disabilities are distributed throughout the population, and that the distinction between those whom we call "disabled" and the majority who are not so regarded is a distinction that is relative rather than absolute. In particular, it is highly relative to the context in which it is used and to the special criteria applicable in that context. In this materialistic age in which we live, the context is far too often the market economy, and the criteria the cash value of the activities in which the person evaluated engages.

Is it possible that we can move to a different context and to different and more adequate criteria? Dare one venture to suggest a more humanistic context in which human beings are valued for their humanity rather than for their contribution to the economy? That would be truly revolutionary, and it would at once bring the benefit of a vast increase in self-esteem for disabled people. Dare

one venture to make the further suggestion that the
context should be not merely humanistic, but that
of a Christian humanism, for I think it is Christianity which most fully protects the integrity of human
beings. Is it not Christianity which offers the best
prospects for human flourishing, especially to those
who feel themselves rejected by society as it currently is? For the great passport to acceptability in
Western society is to hold a job, and the more
highly paid the job is, the more its holder enjoys
the esteem of society. Unfortunately, it is often the
case that those who are considered handicapped or
disabled find that for one reason or another they
cannot find a place in the highly competitive job
structure of modern industry and commerce. It is
true that more consideration is given to them than
was formerly the case, and quite a large number of
employers make an effort to accommodate in their
businesses persons who in one way or another are
perhaps less than 100% efficient. It is also true
that businesses themselves are in competition with
one another, and that they have to be able to rely
on the performance of their work forces. But even
when allowance is made for these facts, it still remains true that such impersonal criteria as profits
and efficiency are the overriding ones. Most people would probably say that a better society would
be one in which human considerations were ac-
corded greater weight, but when it comes down to
making actual decisions, the pressures of the
market economy take over, and those who cannot
fulfill the demands of the market are pushed to the
margins. There is, perhaps, the promise that in

better times (if they ever come) there will be a better deal for the marginalized.

Of course, it is a difficult and also a delicate situation. Disabled people are for the most part unwilling to seek favors or special concessions. They are to be accepted as they are, for the things that they can do and in the knowledge that there are things they cannot do. But, as I said, this is the universal human condition. Virtually everyone has something that he or she can do reasonably well, but we all have things that we cannot do and probably could never learn to do.

But perhaps on touching on the problem of incorporating disabled people into the work force, I have been too ready to accept the idea that one must hold a job in order to have a recognized place in society. That is certainly how it is in the prosperous societies of Europe and North America, governed as they are by the motives of the production and consumption of material goods. But surely many would want to look beyond that kind of society, and certainly those who claim to be Christians would. Karl Marx believed that a person needs work if he is to enjoy dignity and self-esteem, and Marx may well have been right. To be able to work and produce something worthwhile, and then in turn to be rewarded by society for the result of the work, is a satisfying experience, and the more people who can have that experience, the better.

Love as the Passport to Humanity

But even if work is impossible, due to disabilities or even to the lack of opportunity, just being a human person should be a sufficient passport to society. Indeed, one could be enormously efficient at many tasks, and yet be lacking in the most important human qualities. I did say earlier that to lack a particular ability does not abolish or even diminish the humanity of the person concerned. It would surely be impossible to make a list of qualities and say, "These are essential to a human being." One of the few theologians who has written on these questions, David Pailin, remarks: "There is no single set of material values which defines what it is to be fully and properly human."[3] On the other hand, it is perhaps possible to say that when all kinds of admired qualities are present, but when one other most needful quality is lacking, there is a failure to achieve a full humanity. I have in mind the famous words of Paul:

> Though I speak with the tongues of men and of angels, and have not charity, I am become as sounding brass or a tinkling cymbal. And though I have the gift of prophecy, and understand all mysteries and all knowledge, and though I have all faith so that I could move mountains, and have not charity, I am nothing. And though I bestow all my goods to feed the poor, and though I give my body to be burned, and have not charity, it profiteth me nothing. (1 Cor 13: 1-3)

Here, the standards by which the sophisticated and civilized world judges are rejected. Love, not efficiency, is made the supreme test of what is or is not authentically human. Someone may say, is this not far too idealistic? Is this not Paul expecting the end of the present world and already looking forward to the coming of the kingdom of God, in which these new values will indeed be universally valid? But of what relevance is this in our present world, pervaded as it is by materialism, competition, aggression and many other grievous features? Certainly, we do have to be realistic, and acknowledge that Paul's great hymn of love arises from the vision of a society that is light-years away from the kind of societies that we know here on earth. But unless some people have this vision, and unless many more people seek to share in their vision, we shall simply remain stuck where we are. Paul and even Jesus himself seem to speak of a world and of human relationships so different from what we see around us that we are indeed tempted to dismiss them as mere visionaries. But the very fact that in this world of ours such persons have appeared and have opened our eyes to new possibilities which may seem to be even impossibilities is itself a ground of hope. Remember the starting point of our thinking—that the human being does not have set characteristics unchanging for all time, but is constituted by possibilities, and these open out before all of us and stretch as far as our vision can reach.

In the course of this discussion, I have been visualizing limited disabilities. Some of these are severe enough, and they do raise questions for Christian faith. But what about those disabilities of the most severe kind, laying an apparently intolerable burden on those who suffer under them? Is there any word for them, or for those of them who can still hear a word? There are, I think, depths of suffering before which one can only be silent. Anything one might venture to say seems superficial. But when I think of that extreme of helplessness, when every power and every faculty seems to be in abeyance, yet the human reality made in the image of God has not been destroyed, I think of Jesus Christ crucified. He has already been brutally scourged and assaulted. He hangs there, alive but only just. He cannot move his limbs, his body is racked by unimaginable pain. Along with these physical afflictions is the mental and emotional agony. His friends have all gone away; even the Father in heaven seems to have forsaken him. Yet Christ on the cross, a man reduced to uttermost, is manifesting to us the fullness of life and the fullness of love, the very life and love of God. Remember his words in St. John's Gospel: "I, if I be lifted up, will draw all men to me" (Jn 12: 32). The evangelist explains that he said this to show by what death he was to die. So it was when he was lifted up on the cross, in utter helplessness, that Jesus was most truly exalted. He brought the great human possibility of love to its highest pitch, and so even in his suffering he brought humanity itself to its highest moment.

I spoke a moment ago of Jesus' bringing the great human possibility of love and even human nature itself to its highest pitch of being. But in Christian theology, we believe with St. Paul that "God was in Christ, reconciling the world to himself." So it is not only human love, but divine love that is manifested in the self-sacrificing death of Christ. In spite of the traditional doctrine of the divine impassibility, that is to say, the doctrine that God cannot himself be touched by suffering, I think we must believe that if God was in Christ, then God shared in the suffering of Christ. Indeed, God shares in the suffering of all his creatures, including those who suffer through some handicap or disability. I did say earlier that although we say that God is omnipotent, this does not mean that he can do absolutely anything. He acts within the bounds of his own nature, his own rationality and his own love. In bringing into being a creation within which were finite creatures who were nevertheless made in the divine image and called to grow into the divine likeness, God of necessity opened the door to suffering, for that which is finite can never be perfect in the same way as the Infinite has perfection.

If we thought that God had simply created the universe and then left it to evolve on its own, we might feel some resentment at the trials which human beings undergo. But surely that situation is quite transformed when we know that God himself is with us in the suffering of the creation, in the person of the Holy Spirit. Again, it is St. Paul who puts this into words for us:

When we say, "Abba, Father!" it is the Spirit bearing witness with our spirit that we are children of God, and if children, then heirs, heirs of God and fellow heirs with Christ, provided we suffer with him that we may also be glorified with him. . . . We know that the whole creation has been groaning in travail until now; and not only the creation, but we ourselves, who have the first fruits of the Spirit, groan inwardly as we wait for adoption as sons and daughters, the redemption of our bodies. (Rom 8:15-17 and 22-23)

We can then live in patience and hope, knowing that God suffers with us and sustains us in our suffering, and is striving to bring all things to that consummation which he has destined for them.

Notes

1. Pascal, Blaise, *Pensees*, No. 391.

2. Schleiermacher, F., 1988. *On Religion*, Cambridge England: Cambridge University Press.

3. Pailin, D. 1992. *A Gentle Touch: From a Theology of Handicap to a Theology of Human Being*, London: Society for Promoting Christian Knowledge (S.P.C.K.).

The Church and Mentally Handicapped Persons: A Continuing Challenge to the Imagination

Stanley Hauerwas

The presumption behind this paper is that no amount of "tinkering" with seminary education will be sufficient to help seminarians understand those with "disabilities" unless we see how "disabilities" challenge our current ecclesial and theological presumptions. The challenge is accordingly much more radical than simply making the seminary open to another "advocacy group."

The challenge of being as well as caring for those called "mentally handicapped" is to prevent those who wish they never existed or would "just go away" from defining them as "the problem" of mentally handicapped people. It is almost impossible to resist descriptions that make being mentally handicapped "a problem" since those descriptions are set by the power of the "normal." For example, parents who have a mentally handicapped child were often, and sometimes still are, told such a child will be happier "institutionalized." Such roadblocks continue when parents try to get adequate medical care and find often that doctors assume that it would be better for everyone if this child would die. The adversity continues as parents face the hundreds of silent slights contained in the stares of people in grocery stores and service stations, stares that communicate, "Thank God that is not me."

Such roadblocks and slights are destined to get worse as our society seeks and finds ways to eliminate mentally handicapped people. What will happen, for example, if this society starts requiring amniocentesis? The human genome project is a potential threat to people who are mentally handicapped since it will encourage the presumption that people should regulate their sexual and marital behavior to avoid having disabled children. What will our society say to those who decide to challenge the presuppositions that we ought to avoid having mentally handicapped children? Is it possible to envision that society may well put legal and financial penalties on people who decide to have children who are less than "normal?"

Of course, implicit in these projects is the false assumption that most of those with mental handicaps are primarily born rather than made. Thus even if this society decides to eliminate the birth of mentally handicapped children, they will continue to be confronted by those environmentally handicapped—that is, whose condition is the result of pollution, nutritional deficits and poverty rather than genetics. The care of those whose handicap is the result of such environmental causes may even be worse since, on the whole, this society has already decided that such "unfortunate accidents" should not exist.

There are, moreover, roadblocks dealing with adequate education of people who are mentally handicapped. Schools are not set up to handle mentally handicapped students because they do not learn as we learn. Mentally handicapped children are segregated not because they cannot learn but, rather, because they are not like us. Moreover, we fear those who are not like us. It is said that they will slow other children down (and well they might), but it is never thought that they might speed other children up morally.

Faced with such roadblocks and challenges, those who have and care for mentally handicapped people often feel that their most immediate task is to try to overcome the immediate threats. They become advocates of normalization and fight for the "least restrictive environment" for the mentally handicapped persons. These strategies, to be sure, have much to recommend them, but they can too easily become part of the agenda of those who basically want to deny the existence of people who are mentally handicapped. Ask yourself, for example: would you want to be pressured to be normal?

Who is to say what that entails? Since I am a Texan, I would not have the slightest idea what it means to be normal. While I do not disagree with most of the recommendations put forward in the name of normalization, I do worry that that concept does not itself specify what we need to say on behalf of people who are mentally handicapped. Or perhaps better put, what we need to make it possible for them to speak on their own behalf.

Particularly disturbing is how our response to challenges of living with people who are mentally handicapped tends to put the burden of care entirely on the family. Our society seems to say, "Your luck was bad, and now you are stuck with this kid. We will help you so as long as you do not ask for too much." Therefore, the family becomes the only agent representing the mentally handicapped child since there is absolutely no one else to represent them.

Many of us who care for mentally handicapped people then get caught in contradictions that seem unavoidable. For example, in the interest of supporting the family in their care of their child, we maintain that the family has all rights for their mentally handicapped child. The family can best serve the interest of the child on the assumption that parents know best the child's needs.

However, we then feel at a loss when we encounter families who do not want their child. Those who refuse to provide basic medical care for a baby with Down syndrome when there is need of further surgery is a dramatic example of this problem. As a result, we have institutions filled with mentally handicapped people who are there because they have been abandoned by the only people this society thinks can care for them—their parents.

Christian Imagination as Response

These examples challenge our imaginations concerning how we are to be with mentally handicapped people. What has gone wrong is not that we are people lacking good will, but that we simply do not know how to care. We need the challenge of real people who will teach us how to care. Such people really are the imagination of a community, for we must remember that imagination is not something we have in our minds. Rather, the imagination is a pattern of possibilities forced on community by its stories and correlative commitments. Necessities force us out of our paths of least resistance and, as a result, make us more likely to be communities that know how to care for one another.

Our imaginations, when driven by little more than the logic of our desires, can quite easily lead us astray. As Christians, this should not surprise us since we have learned that those aspects of our lives which offer the greatest resources for good also offer the greatest resources for evil. This is why human imagination, like any other human capacity, must be ordered by something more determinative.

For Christians, that something which is more determinative is both the story of who God has called us to be and our concrete attempts to embody that faithfully. For a community with such a self-understanding, imagination is not a power that somehow exists "in the mind," but is a pointer to a community's constant willingness to expose itself to the innovations required by its convictions about who God is. Similarly, the world is seen differently when construed by such an imaginative community, for the world is not simply *there*, always ready to be known. Rather it is known well only when known through the practices and habits of community constituted by a truthful story.

The Christian imagination forces us to acknowledge that the world is different than it seems. This reality requires Christians to be willing to explore imaginative possibilities in a way not required of those who do not share the narratives and practices that both make us Christian and shape our worldview. Of course, stating the matter in this way is dangerous, for it can easily be interpreted to mean that Christians refuse to acknowledge the world as it "really is." In other words, we open ourselves to the charge that by failing to live in the world "as it really is," our view of the world arises out of fantasy or illusion.

Yet Christians hold that the so-called "world-as-it-really-is" is itself fantasy. Therefore, we must learn to live imaginatively, seeing what is not easily seen, if we are to embody faithfully the character of the God we worship. For example, Christians are well aware of how easy it is to live as if the world has no Creator. In short, it is easy to live as if we, as well as "nature," had no purpose other than to survive. But to live in such a way is not to live in the world "as it is." For to live in the world "as it is" is to be the kind of people who can see that everything has been created to glorify its Creator—including people who are mentally handicapped. To fail to live in such a way is to deny the way the world "is." This is why Christians believe that imagination formed by the storied practices of the Church constitutes the ultimate realism.

"Realism" is often used in epistemological contexts to denote the position whose advocates believe that there are objects which can be known "in and of themselves." Realists often contrast their views with those who emphasize the importance of the imagination, associating the latter with fantasy. Imagination is fiction, but knowledge, it is alleged, describes the world "as it is." There is no question that common usage underwrites this kind of distinction between knowledge and imagination, i.e., "It's all in her imagination." But as Garret Green observes, it is also the case that people think imagination is essential for helping us know what would otherwise go unnoticed. Thus we often praise people who demonstrate "insight and imagination."[1]

There is much to be said for people, like Green, who want to rehabilitate imagination as a mode of knowing that is essential to how Christians think about the world. According to Green, "Imagination is the means by which we are able to present anything not directly accessible, including *both* the world of the imaginary *and* recalcitrant aspects of the real world; it is the medium of fiction as well as of fact."[2] Imagination, therefore, seems to be central to the kind of claims Christians make about God.

However, one problem with proposals such as Green's is that such accounts of imagination are so abstract and disembodied. This is partly because they accept the assumption that the status of imagination is fundamentally an epistemological issue divorced from the practices of particular communities. On the contrary, the Christian imagination is constituted by practices such as nonviolence and learning how to be present to and how to be with people who are mentally handicapped: hopefully we know them by name, not as mentally handicapped people but as Anna and Boyce, our sister and brother in Christ.

Children, the Church, and Mentally Handicapped People

Of course, learning to live joyfully with the Anna's and the Boyce's draws on the resources of other practices that sustain their presence. For example, consider an issue that at first may seem quite foreign to the question of how we should care for those with mental handicaps—namely, why we have children in the first place. I often used to begin a course in the theology and ethics of marriage at the University of Notre Dame with the question, "What reason would you give for yourself or someone else having a child?" Few students had thought about the question, and their responses were less than convincing: that is, children are to manifest their love for one another, as a hedge against loneliness, for fun, and/or to please grandparents. Often, one student would finally say that they wanted to have children to make the world better. The implicit assumption behind this reason for having children was that they would have superior children who, having been brought up with the right kind of training, would be enabled to solve the world's problems.

Such reasoning often appears morally idealistic. However its limitations can be quickly revealed by showing its implications for mentally handicapped people. People who want to have superior children in order to make the world better are deeply threatened by mentally handicapped people. If children are part of a progressive story about the necessity to make the world better, these children do not seem to fit. At best they can only be understood as deserving existence insofar as our care of them makes us better people.

Such attitudes about having children reveal a society with a deficient moral imagination. It is an imagination that is correlative to a set of practices about having and caring for children that results in the destruction of mentally handicapped babies.

The fundamental mistake regarding parenting in our society is the assumption that biology makes parents. In the absence of any good reason for having children, people assume they have responsibilities to their children because they are biologically "theirs." Lost is any sense of how parenting is an office of a community rather than a biologically described role.

In contrast, Christians assume, given the practice of baptism, that parenting is the vocation of everyone in the church, whether they are married or single. Childbearing for Christians is part of the church's commitment to hospitality of the stranger since we believe that the church is sustained by God across generations by witness rather than by ascribed biological destinies. Therefore, everyone in the church has a parental role, whether they have biological children or not.

For Christians, children are neither the entire responsibility nor property of the parents. Parents are given responsibility for particular children insofar as they pledge faithfully to bring up the child, but the community ultimately stands over against the parents, reminding the parents that the child has a standing in the community separate from the parent. Therefore, how mentally handicapped children are received in such a community should be strikingly different than how they are received in the wider society. For the whole burden of the care for such a child does not fall on the parents, but rather the child is now seen as a gift to the whole community.

At the very least, this means that the church should be the place where the parents and the mentally handicapped child can be without apologizing, without the stares, and without the silent condemnations. If anyone acts as if we ought to be ashamed for having such a child among us, then they will have to take on the whole church. For this is not just this set of parents' child, but this child is the child of the whole church, one whom the church would not choose to be without. Moreover, as this child grows to be an adult, she or he is expected to care as well as to be cared for as a member of the church.[4]

Such a child may add special burdens to the community, but on the average not more than any child. For every child, mentally handicapped or not, always comes to this community challenging our presuppositions. Some children just challenge us more than others as they reveal the limits of our practices. Christians are people who rejoice when we receive such challenges, for we know them to be the source of our imaginations through which God provides us with the skills to have children in a dangerous world. The church is constituted by a people who have been surprised by God, and accordingly know that we live through such surprises.

The church, therefore, is that group of people who are willing to have their imagination constantly challenged through the necessities created by children, some of whom may be mentally handicapped. The church is constituted by those people who can take the time in a world crying with injustice to have children, some of whom may turn out to be mentally handicapped. We can do that because we believe this is the way God would rule this world. For we do not believe that the world can be made better if such children are left behind.

Implications of Imaginative Ideology

I am aware that this is an over-idealized view of the church's treatment of mentally handicapped children. But I believe I am indicating the potential contained in common Christian practice. Moreover, the presence of mentally handicapped people helps Christians to rediscover the significance of the common, because this presence calls into question some of our most cherished assumptions about what constitutes Christianity.

For example, often in Christian communities a great emphasis is placed on the importance of "belief." In attempts to respond to critiques of Christian theology in modernity, the importance of intellectual commitments is often taken to be the hallmark of participation in the church. What it means to be Christian is equivalent to being "ultimately concerned" about the existential challenges of human existence and so on. Yet the more emphasis that is placed upon the importance of belief as the hallmark of individuals in the church, the more those with mental handicaps are marginalized. For what those with mental handicaps challenge the church to remember is that what saves is not our own personal existential commitments but being a member of a body constituted by practices more determinative than my "personal" commitment.

I suspect this is the reason why mentally handicapped people are often better received in more "liturgical" traditions—that is, traditions that know what God is doing through the community's ritual is more determinative than what any worshiper brings to or receives from the ritual. After all, the God worshipped is the Spirit, who cannot be subject to human control. The liturgy of the church is ordered to be open to such wildness by its hospitality to that Spirit. What mentally handicapped people might do to intrude into that order is nothing compared to what the Spirit has done and will continue to do. Indeed their presence just may well be the embodiment of the Spirit.

Nowhere is the individualistic and rationalistic character of modern Christianity better revealed than in the practice of Christian education. For example, religious education is often the attempt to "teach" people the doctrine of the Christian faith separate from any determinative practices. Yet we know that salvation cannot come from knowing this or that, but rather by participating in a community through which our lives are constituted by a unity more profound than our individual needs. From such a perspective, mentally handicapped people and children are not accidental to what the church is about, but without their presence the church has no way to know it is church—that the church is body. If the word is preached and the sacraments served without the presence of mentally handicapped people, then it may be that we are less than the body of Christ.

Mentally handicapped people are reminders that belief and faith are not individual matters. Rather, faith names the stance of the church as a political body via the world. We are not members of a church because we know what we believe, but we are members of a church because we need the whole church to believe for us. Often, if not most of the time, I find that I come to be part of the community that worships God not as a believer or as a faithful follower of Christ, but as someone who is just "not there." I may not be a disbeliever, but I am by no means a believer either. By being present to others in church, I find that I am made more than I would otherwise be—I am made one in the faith of the church—my body is constituted by the body called church.

People who are mentally handicapped remind us that their condition is the condition of us all insofar as we are faithful followers of Christ. The church is not a collection of individuals but rather a people on a journey who are known by the time they take to help one another along the way. We know that God would not have us try to make the world better if that means leaving those with mental handicaps behind.[5] They are the way we must learn to walk in the journey that God has given us. They are God's imagination, and to the extent we become one with them, we become God's imagination for the world.

Of course, worshipping with mentally handicapped people can be no easy matter. Such worship can be quite disorderly since we are never sure what they may or may not do. They create a "wildness" that frightens because they are not easily domesticated.

Yet exactly to the extent that they create the unexpected, they remind us that the God we worship is not easily domesticated. For in worship the church is made vulnerable to a God who would rule this world not by coercion but through the unpredictability of love. Christians thus learn that people with mental handicaps are not among us because we need someone to be the object of charity, but because without these brothers and sisters in Christ we call "retarded," we cannot know what it means rightly to worship God.

So through the prism of worship, Christians discover mentally handicapped people as brothers and sisters in Christ. They are not seen as victims of our society. For their great strength is their refusal to be victimized by the temptations to become a victim. Through their willingness to be present in church, they provide the church with the time to be church. We thus learn that we can take the time for someone who does not talk well to read the Scriptures. We can take the time to walk slowly together to the Communion table when one of our own does not walk well or at all. We can take the time to design our places of gathering so that they are open to many who would otherwise not be able to be there. We can take the time to be a people open to children who will always distract us from the projects that seem so promising for making the world "better."

A community formed imaginatively by the presence of mentally handicapped people should, however, provide ways to respond to the challenges and roadblocks mentioned at the beginning. For if the wider society lacks the basis for knowing how to care for those with a mental handicap, it does so because it is devoid of examples to help it spur its imagination. What we need to exhibit is that it is not simply the question of how to "care" for mentally handicapped people. It is not that those with mental handicaps are among us to be helped, although like all of us they will need help, but rather that by their being among us, we learn how we are all more able to be a community.

It is interesting, for example, how quickly communities forget how certain practices designed for the "handicapped" become accepted as ways of life for everyone. Thus a study at the University of Kansas asked why slopes had been put into sidewalks. Most respondents said that they thought that they were there to make bicycling easier. So the access for disabled people becomes an opportunity for the whole community.

Certainly the ignorance and cruelty of the wider society toward mentally handicapped people need to be constantly challenged. But more important is the witness of those who have learned that it is not simply a matter of caring but of learning to be with people who are "different." Only when we learn how to be with those different from us can we learn to accept the love that each of us needs to sustain a community capable of worshipping God. It should not be surprising, therefore, that Christians may well be seen in the future as a people who have learned how to be with mentally handicapped people. We may accordingly be thought very odd indeed if our society continues in the direction of the threats discussed above. Yet we believe that nothing could be more significant for a world that assumes that God has not given us the timeful imaginations to be with those whom we call "mentally handicapped."

Notes

1. Green, G., *Imagining God: Theology and the Religious Imagination.* New York: Harper and Row, 1989, p. 63.

2. Green, p. 66.

3. I think there is a profound relationship between Christian nonviolence and the joy Christians are to learn from mentally handicapped people. Each forces us to be what we otherwise could not become. For example, pacifists are often challenged with, "What would you do if . . .?" in the hopes that the Christian imagination will be extinguished in the name of "realism." Yet as John Howard Yoder points out, such a question assumes we are trapped by an inescapable determinism: "I

alone have a decision to make. My relationship with the other person in this situation is at bottom one which unfolds mechanically. The attacker is preprogrammed to do the worst evil he can—or at least the evil he has fixed on his mind. He is not expected to make any other decisions or act in any other way." *What Would You Do?: A Serious Answer to a Standard Question*, Scottsdale, Pennsylvania: Herald Press, 1983, p. 14. Yet the Christian, exactly because we believe our existence, just like the existence of the mentally handicapped person, is a gift, gives us alternatives to such a deterministic world. For Christians, the "real world" is that constituted by the community formed by a crucified yet resurrected Jesus. That resurrection reminds us that we do not live in a world determined by violence, but in a world constituted by God's nonviolence exemplified in the cross of Jesus. Such nonviolence is made possible by the moral skills of this community which seeks to embody the character of this God, skills which constitute cracks in the ubiquitous violence that characterizes the so-called "real world." Such imagination is not fantasy if God is the God of the resurrection miracle. Just as that God will not have "peace" created through violence, neither will God have our lives made "better" through the elimination of the retarded. For further reflection on the relation of the care of the weak and non-violence, see Philip Kenneson's and my, "The Church and/as God's Non-Violent Imagination," *Pro Ecclesia* 1, 1 (Fall, 1992) pp. 76-88. I have included some paragraphs of that essay in this chapter. I am indebted to Professor Kenneson for joining me in the writing of them.

4.   For a wonderful account of the ability of disabled children to lead Christian lives, see Brett Webb-Mitchell, *God Plays Piano Too: The Spiritual Lives of Disabled Children*, New York: Crossroads, 1993.

5.   For a more extended account of this sense of time, see my *Christian Existence Today: Essays on Church, World, and Living In-Between*, Durham: Labyrinth Press, 1988, pp. 253-266.   The most insightful account of my views about time are made by Philip Kenneson in his, "Taking Time for the Trivial: Reflections on Yet Another Book from Hauerwas," *Asbury Theological Journal*, 45, 1 (Spring, 1990), pp. 65-74.